The Whistle

A True Story of Friendship

Pat Heller & Peggy Vogelsinger

The Whistle

ISBN: 978-1-935125-77-8

Illustrated by Virginia Fordice

Printed in the United States of America

To order additional copies of this book, go to:
www.rp–author.com/whistle

*(An order form for the **Whistle** is on the last page.)*

Robertson Publishing
59 N. Santa Cruz Avenue, Suite B
Los Gatos, California 95030 USA
(888) 354-5957 • www.RobertsonPublishing.com

This story is dedicated to all those
who have lost parts of themselves... and found something very special...

This is a story about whistles and friendship.
Really, a story about one friendship and one whistle...but we hope by
telling our story it will become a story about many whistles and many friendships.

A long time ago, two very best friends, who lived close to each other, had to move apart. On their last day together they sat on Peggy's front porch while box after box, sofa after chair and too many toys to count were loaded onto a big red truck bound for another home and another state.

Pat, who stayed behind, asked, "What will I do without you?"

Peggy replied, *"If you ever need me, just whistle."* She handed Pat a bright shiny whistle on a long silver chain. Pat slipped it around her neck, they hugged goodbye and both cried all the way home—Pat to her old house and Peggy to her new one.

Years passed. Birthdays came and went. Kids grew.

They moved to yet other states. Every once in a while, Pat would open her mailbox and find another whistle, a *special* reminder that somewhere was someone who would always be there for her if she just whistled.

They wrote. They called. They laughed and, often, tears would accompany their phone calls. They even snuck a few precious visits into their way too hectic lives. In all this time Pat never needed to whistle for her friend.

Over the years the collection of whistles grew. They quietly hung on a hook, collecting dust, and always were a gentle sign of the gift of their friendship.

One lovely sunny day, Pat was driving down a street she rarely took and saw an accident. A really bad accident. Stopping her car, Pat jumped out to see if she could offer help—as all good people do. She found what a woman was screaming for her to find. She stayed in the middle of the street, as cars drove around her, protecting what she first thought was a plastic part of a doll. Yes, she had thoughts of wanting to leave when she saw that this part was *not* plastic but real. She even thought about running away but an inner voice told her she must stay to keep safe what was between her feet. Kind people directed the traffic around her. Soon she heard the loud sirens of the fire trucks, the police cars and the ambulance coming to help. Now, she could leave.

Tired and shaken, Pat went home and called Peggy. She listened to the story of the accident and knew that Pat was terribly upset and needed her. There was silence after Pat stopped talking and then Peggy said, "I do not think this story is finished. You must find out what happened to the little girl who was in the accident. You are whistling for me, and I think we should find out what this story means…for you and for her and for us."

Weeks passed and there was no way that Pat could know what happened to the little girl. She simply waited and listened for news. She trusted Peggy's words and believed that in time she would meet the little girl again. One day a call came. Strangely, it happened to be a day when Pat needed a blessing because there was great sadness in her own life.

"Hello, I want to thank you for being our hero. You will always be a member of our family for being there when we needed you," said a gentle voice, the mother of the little girl. Before they said goodbye, they arranged for Pat to come and visit them.

As Pat was leaving for her visit, she saw something sparkling. The whistles on the hook were catching the sunlight through the window. That same inner voice told her that she should wear a whistle. Pat chose the brightest, flashiest of all the whistles and put it around her neck.

And, she was remembering Peggy…

Pat was concerned about what to say to the little girl as she walked up to the front door. She was worried that she might cry and knew that she must not frighten the little girl. The little girl was still recovering from the many surgeries following the accident. Pat knocked on the door and it was opened by the mother. She said, "Please come in." They hugged a long time before they walked down the hall to the little girl's bedroom.

The little girl was in her grandmother's arms trying to use her hand that had been injured in the accident. Pat knelt down to the floor so that she could see her face. What she saw was a smiling face whose eyes were fixed on the whistle. Pat said, "Hello, little one—I am the lady who met you long before I met you." They talked a short time about how that had happened. Mostly, Pat told the little girl about the story of her whistle, of being able to simply whistle when she needed her friend.

Again, the inner voice seemed to speak to Pat. She suddenly took off her whistle and gave it to the little girl. If a face can look like sunshine, Pat was certain that she saw a glowing and bright one. Pat said, "I will let you borrow my whistle so that you can use it when you need help or when you need someone to hold you, to talk to you, to listen to you… *If you ever need anything, just whistle!*"

The visits between Pat and the little girl continued week after week, month after month. During this time the little girl had to have many more surgeries. These were not easy times for the little girl and her family. They had a lot of love and caring for one another which gave them strength for the healing that was happening.

For each visit Pat brought a different whistle—and the little girl whistled and whistled. She whistled for her mother, her father, her brother. She whistled for all those who were around her to help her heal. The little girl never asked to keep any of the "borrowed" whistles because she knew they were only on loan. For you see, whistles like friends cannot be given away. They can only be shared. Pat promised the little girl that Peggy, although living far away, would someday send her a special whistle of her own.

But, this story is not yet finished…

One day when Pat came to visit with another whistle, the door flew open before she could even knock. The little girl was laughing and cried out, "LOOK!" She was wearing a different but similar whistle. It was not Pat's borrowed one.

"Where did you get that whistle?" asked Pat.

The little girl told her the story. Since she was beginning to feel better and stronger, her father took her on an outing to the farmer's market. While walking around, the little girl heard whistling and followed the sound. She saw a smiling lady selling whistles. The lady was very kind and told her that she had been making whistles all her life and sending them all over the world. The little girl's father bought her a whistle with painted hearts. Now, she had her very own whistle.

Pat was puzzled. She said, "How odd. Your whistle is exactly like some of those that are hanging on my hook." Pat felt that she must find the whistle lady. She found her stall at the farmer's market and discovered that, indeed, many of the whistles that had been coming for years from Peggy were made by her.

The little girl had found a whistle of her own from the very same lady!

Though hanging on a hook they may have appeared to be only whistles, Pat and Peggy have known that these were *special* whistles. They were reminders that over the many years and the distance between them, Pat had Peggy and Peggy had Pat tucked into their hearts. The whistles had always served to help them whenever their lives needed this reminder of the gift of a forever friend.

This part of the story is all told.

If you have someone, somewhere, who always seems to be there for you, give them a special whistle. Then, someday, you will be able to tell your own story of how a simple whistle not only changed your life, but someone else's as well.

For Peggy and Pat look at their friendship and whistles differently now. They know their story of friendship will never be finished because maybe a hero is like being a friend. Like friendship, heroism is about the willingness to be there for someone in life's many ways, when life brings difficulties and joys—and about the courage and generosity and strength of a forever heart.

Pat Heller & Peggy Vogelsinger

Peggy Vogelsinger

After being raised on a dairy farm in central Illinois alongside two brothers, Peggy graduated from Knox College and spent several years teaching. She became a stay at home Mom when her two sons were born, one in Chicago and one in Detroit. It was in the suburbs of Detroit where she met Pat while the husbands were finishing school. She began a "career" of community volunteering in Rochester, Minnesota and Peoria, Illinois which eventually led her to seminary in Milwaukee. After graduating from McCormick Theological Seminary, she became an ordained Presbyterian minister and now lives in Bloomington, Illinois. Although retired from full time ministry so she can spend more time with her family, including granddaughters in Naperville and San Francisco, she loves to travel, speak on life and faith, and write. To Peggy life is an adventure, changing with the dawn and joys of each new day.

Pat Heller

Pat received her BFA from the University of Southern California and taught art in junior high school. While her husband completed his medical training in Detroit, Pat's friendship with Peggy began and has continued for over 37 years. Establishing a medical clinic on the island of Roatan, Honduras, Pat and her family fulfilled their dream and lived as islanders for one year. When the family returned to Los Gatos, California, Pat earned her graduate degree in social work and practiced as a psychotherapist. Now retired, she is a community volunteer and, also, volunteers her poodle, Thor, as a therapy dog. Her ongoing passion is her family and friends and practicing not being lazy about the present—taking life as it comes and always being amazed at the infinite joys, surprises and challenges that unfold.

Virginia Fordice ~ Artist/Illustrator

Virginia Fordice grew up in Saratoga, California. At the age of four with her Christmas crayons, she painted her first mural, thirty feet, along the stone wall which marked her driveway. Now, she creates large works in leaded glass and paintings in watercolor, oil and acrylic. Visitors are welcome by appointment to her Santa Cruz Mountain Studio. P.O. Box 628, Boulder Creek, California, 95006.

Joan Anderson ~ Artist/Potter

Joan grew up in Los Angeles and played in the mud. She liked making mud bowls, and that's how it all started. As a potter Joan has created her colorful whistles for many years. Her attention to detail highlights the unique quality of each whistle, and no two are alike. Joan has sold her beautiful handcrafted whistles locally as well as internationally. Her studio is located in Oakland, California.

Acknowledgments:

We are most appreciative to the many who have supported our efforts to tell this story. Thank you to Jan Parsons and Linda Sibley who gave us guidance and encouragement. In a very personal way we offer our deepest gratitude to our children—especially, to David for his keen eye with his camera and to Matthew for his "eagle" eye in reviewing our writing. A special thanks to the men in our lives—who never stood in the way of our friendship. We have been inspired by the Rix and Thomsen families who have shown the strength of family love and inspired others.

Handcrafted whistles.

Whistle Order Form

Name:_____

Address:_____

City:_____

State:_____ Zip Code:_____

Country:_____

Phone:_____

Description	Quantity	Total
Whistle	1	6.50
Cost includes first class shipping and handling, plus tax.		

Limited to one whistle for each book purchased. Photocopies of this form will not be accepted.

Please note that these beautiful custom designed handcrafted whistles are NOT TOYS.
The whistle and cord could be a choking or strangling hazard for a young child. Think JEWELRY!

Please enclose check or money order with this order form.

Make Checks/Money orders Payable To: Peggy Vogelsinger

Mail To:

Peggy Vogelsinger
1314 Crown Court
Bloomington, IL 61704

CUT HERE

LaVergne, TN USA
27 April 2010
180673LV00002B